T0086046

# I'LL FLY AWAY

POEMS BY

Rudy Francisco

© 2020 by Rudy Francisco

◇

Published by Button Poetry / Exploding Pinecone Press
Minneapolis, MN 55403 | http://www.buttonpoetry.com

◇

All Rights Reserved
Manufactured in the United States of America
Cover design: Nikki Clark
ISBN 978-1-943735-69-3

# Contents

*"One glad morning,*
*When this life is over*
*I'll*


*Fly away."*

I'LL FLY AWAY

## Mama Saba asks

"What's the word for that
in English?"

And there I am,
trying to catch the breeze
with a butterfly net.

I fumble through
the only language I know
and find everything
but an answer.

Eventually, I give up and say,
"I don't think there is one."

English is the shiniest hammer
I own, but it's also
the only thing in my toolbox.

I use it all the time,
but there is so much
it cannot do.

# Nolexi *noun*

no · lex · i  |  \ nō-lek-si \

## Definition of *nolexi*:

**1**  : a word or phrase that does not exist or has no direct translation in a particular language

The following words do not currently exist in the English language, but they should:

Nolexi
Amoriode
Mortaprime
Culi
Coamplify
Repensist

## This is how I scare the dirt

away from the coffin,

puff out my chest
and intimidate the soil;

this is how
I reverse my own burial.

I ask,
"What do we tell the god of death?"
and the poem says, "Not today."

Sometimes,
a pen

is also a shovel.

# Amoriode *verb*

a · mor · i · o · de  |  \ a-mȯ-rī-ōd \

## Definition of *amoriode*:

**1**     : the act or an instance of dying while doing an activity you love

## Legend has it

when J Dilla was admitted to the hospital,
he took his production equipment with him
and made instrumentals out of everything
inside his body that wasn't ready to die.
The last thing he did on this earth was make music.

How beautiful it is to grind yourself into sand,
offer the grain of you to anyone willing to listen,

hoping they will carry your debris
into places you'll never go.

# Mortaprime *noun*

mort · a · prime  |  \ mȯr-tə-prīm \

## Definition of *mortaprime*:

1    : one who dies too soon
2    : an individual who passes away at a young age


# Culi *noun*

cu · li  |  \ kü-lē \

## Definition of *culi*:

1    : a gifted young person who lives in a poverty-stricken area
2    : the kid in the hood that everyone believes is special

## And maybe we all know a "Ricky"

Someone who will emerge from nothing
like the 1st song on a good album—

A dandelion the neighborhood holds
in the air, hoping
a gust will catch the boy
long enough for him
to land somewhere better.

We grab violence by the collar,
and say,
"Anybody but him."

We offer O-Dog for Cane,
Caesar in exchange for Ruby,

but sometimes negotiations fail.
There seems to be a language barrier.

# Coamplify *verb*

co · am · pli · fy  |  \ kō-am-plə-fī \

## Definition of *coamplify*:

1   : to celebrate the life of someone who has passed away
2   : a mass movement where people around the world continues the legacy of one who has died

## What I know is this

a runner doesn't always cross
the finish line,

but a baton can look like
a microphone depending on
how you hold it.

I know that a marathon
can become a relay
as long as there is someone
willing to finish the race.

I know that a victory lap
isn't over until the music stops.

I know that a person is still alive,
if you remember to say their name.


Nipsey.

# Repensist *noun*

re · pen · sist  |  \ ri-pen-sist \

## Definition of *repensist*:

**1**   : a period of time when a relationship is over, but neither party has realized it

## My parents

were in a long distance
relationship for over 30 years,
and they lived in the same house.

I learned you can
be right next to someone but
also 1,000 miles away from
them without asking geography
its opinion.

Often, the space between 2 people
can be measured by the number
of times they look at each other

and feel nothing.

## Divorce is a stubborn grease fire

a salivating mouth that still holds
an appetite after swallowing
the kitchen.

10 years ago, I watched
a greedy inferno steal
the wedding ring right
off my mother's finger.

To this day, there is still
a relentless shadow on her hand.

The teeth marks of
a 30-year promise left on a stove
we all thought he turned off.

## Love can be
## a reckless child

My heart, a jungle gym
with a pulse.

Maybe we meant all
the things we said
to each other when
we were happy,

but maybe
it was recess.

The bell rang,
but I just didn't hear it.

**Perhaps I told you
I was leaving**

because it was
the only way you
would notice my absence.

I

The following words do not currently exist in the English language, but they should:

Relin
Mendle
Bresil
Beldin
Grusic
Felenter
Odit
Kelvet
Selk

# Relin *noun*

re · lin  |  \ rel-in \

## Definition of *relin*:

**1**    : an unshakeable urge to go somewhere that may or may not exist

# I'll Fly Away (Erasure)

By Albert E. Brumley

Some

shadows  have

prison bars

and

joy

# Mendle *verb*

men · dle  |  \ men-dəl \

## Definition of *mendle*:

**1**    : to do or say nothing when one knows they are being lied to

## The poem where I lie about everything

I'm 6'2,
I weigh 225 lbs. and
I know what you're thinking.
The answer's no, I don't
like basketball.

Yes, the way my parents look at each other
reminds me that love still exits.

Yes, I love swimming,
yes, I'm an only child, and
they are still married.

Exists.
That was a typo.

Yes, my grandmother is still alive.
Yes, I'm fine; yes, I'm always fine.
No, I'm not just saying that so
you'll leave me alone.

Yes, I'm happy. I smile so much
my face hurts. Yes, that is the only
pain I'm familiar with. Yes,

when people say, "good luck,"
I laugh and tell them I'm a rabbit's foot
wrapped in a 4-leaf clover.

Yes, when someone says,
"have a good day,"
I say, "too late . . . already happening."
My eyes? Oh, allergies.
My hands? They shake like this

all the time, the doctor
says "It's normal. No big deal,
just ignore it." Yes,

I'm comfortable talking about my feelings.
Yes, ask me anything.

Yes, I'm lovable.
No, I'm not lonely.
No, I'm not exhausted.
No, I'm not under a lot of pressure.
No.
No.
No.
Yes,

I slept really well last night.
I woke up around 7,
made a breakfast,

I felt guilty,

then went for a run.

## Most of what I know

I've learned from falling,
from placing the brighter side
of my hands against the earth
and pressing until vertical.

The ground has taught me
more about flight

than the sky ever could.

# Bresil *verb*

bre · sil  |  \ brez-əl \

Definition of *bresil*:

**1**    : to miss someone that you see all the time


# Beldin *noun*

bel · din  |  \ bel-din \

Definition of *beldin*:

**1**    : a situation where a person who is always helping other people is in need of help but doesn't know who or how to ask for it

## Sometimes I'm the mess

Sometimes I'm the broom—
on my hardest days,
I have to be both.

## Drowning Fish

During the winter of 2015,
the residents of Hampton Bay, Long Island
woke up to what they say was the worst smell
they had ever experienced.

Mysteriously, overnight,
1,000 fish had died in the canal.

After thorough analysis, they found
that the oxygen levels in the water were too low

and all the fish had drowned.

Upon hearing the news, many had questions:
"How does a fish drown?
"Don't they have gills?"
"Don't they have fins and tails?"
They said things like,
"Aren't they built to survive that environment?"

And perhaps,
this is the best analogy for my depression.

This angry deity,
this jealous God,

this thirsty shadow that wrings my joy like a dishrag,
turns every conversation into a conveyor belt
that always begins with the phrase,
"You look tired today."

To be honest,
getting out of bed has become a magic trick,
and I am probably the worst magician I know.

This sadness is the only clean shirt I have left,
and my washing machine has been broken for months.

When people ask me how I'm doing,
I want to say,
"My daughter is 3-years-old, and I'm still
not sure if I'm a good father."

I wanna say,
"My dad has dementia. There might be a day
when I walk in the room and he doesn't recognize me,
and I've always wanted us to start all over,
but I guess you have to be careful what you ask for."
I guess when you pray for something,
you have to be a little more specific.

I wanna say,
"Crickets have been known to eat their own wings,
and I too have a tendency to destroy what
helps me get off the ground."

I really wanna say,
"I'm kinda fucked up right now."
But that's not a polite answer.

So, instead I pretend that it's Halloween;
I jack-o'-lantern my face into something acceptable,
and I tell others I'm fine until it sounds like the truth.

But, sometimes
there is a "help me" chained to the ankle of an "I'm doing ok"

Sometimes,
"I'm fine," is the easiest way to say,
"I don't want to talk about it."

Sometimes,
all the oxygen in the room becomes water.
I feel like I'm sinking to the bottom,
like I'm running out of air,
but I promised myself that I won't be
another drowning fish.

I will NOT die in this canal.
*Take a deep breath. Relax.*
*The human body will naturally float.*
So, I breathe.
And I tell myself that it's gonna be ok—
I panic.
But I tell myself that it's going to be ok—
And I cry.
but I tell myself that it's going to be ok—
Because I know,
there's a version of me somewhere in the future.

He's looking at this moment right here
and saying, "Rudy, thank you for not giving up on us."

Yesterday, while I was reading,
I saw a run-on sentence and I thought
"You know . . . it could've ended right there,
but it found a reason to just keep going."

I smiled and I said,

"Same."

## Afterwards

One time, while I was
running errands, my car
decided to change occupations.

I assume it saw a couch
and said, "I wanna try that,"
which is to say it stopped moving
at an intersection
during rush hour.

I had it towed to a mechanic,
and he said, "it's something small,
comeback in an hour."

60 minutes later, I was driving to
my next destination. Now I know
there is something after the breakdown.

## 2009 (Erasure)
By Mac Miller

I

take a breath

and

the light      in

me

Isn't

high

But

I do  shine

inside            .

I'm smilin'

because

I

mind my business

I carry my

scared

heart

But

I don't panic

## Here I am today

A breath
that doesn't mind
repeating itself.

Living proof
that sometimes
you plan a funeral,

but a birthday party
shows up instead.

## I wish you a checkered flag

a trophy, an endless ribbon,
and the kind of victory
that muffles the voice
inside of you that says,
"You don't deserve this."

I'm rooting for you

because I know the sun
is not stingy with its rays
and has enough light
to go around.

A flame has no desire
to hold on to its own heat
and doesn't mind warming
multiple hands at once.

"You can't flex on me
if I'm rooting for you."

# Grusic *verb*

gru · sic  |  \ gru-sik \

## Definition of *grusic*:

1    : to be mad at someone for so long you don't remember why
2    : to harbor feelings of hostility without recalling the origin

## I once held on to a grudge

for so long, I forgot how
the conflict actually started.

I let the anger build an
entire city in my hands,
and I was the mayor
for more years than
I'm comfortable admitting.

Since then, I've realized
that this kind of rage
is not worth its carry,

and forgiveness is a little
hard to find, but it's the only
town I want to live in.

It's quiet here

and real estate is cheaper.

# **Felenter** *noun*

fe · len · ter | \ fe-len-tər \

## Definition of *felenter*:

**1**   : one who finds joy in things that people believe to be mundane

## I want the kind of happiness

that you can smell in my clothes,
and a smile so big, you can still
see it when I'm walking
in the opposite direction.

I want to laugh so loud,
my demons pack their belongings
and decide to move.

So these days, I try to take
the most mundane things,

like waking up or doing laundry,

and challenge myself
to carve a small celebration
into every single one.

# **Odit** *noun*

o · dit  |  \ ō-dit \

## Definition of *odit*:

**1**　: a person who has never met you but doesn't like you

## There are people

that you don't know,
who dislike you
for things you never did.

There are people
who start wars but hide
the declaration under
their breath for years.

They see you coming,
stare from a safe distance,
and launch a fleet of ships

using only a glance.

# Kelvet *noun*

kel · vet  |  \ kel-vet \

## Definition of *kelvet*:

**1**    : the joy that is received from blocking a person on social media

## Ode to the block button

They say, "Never look
a gift horse in the mouth."

They will tell you,
"A bird in the hand is
worth 2 in the bush."

They will remind you
of how tragic it is to
block your own blessings.

But what they don't say
is how the block can
also be the blessing,

especially when
used at the right time.
There you are,
tucked into the corner
of the screen,

never asking to be the center
of attention, but always
letting me know that you
are available, and
what is a friend but someone
who shows up when called upon?

Ready to tell the trolls
who I'm not,

what I don't have the energy for
and won't be dealing with today.

At times, social media
can be an entire country
and you are The Secretary of Defense,

Minister of
Who Are You Talking To,

a reminder that
sometimes the best response
is nothing at all:

a blank screen that says,
"User not found."

## Have you ever noticed

how much water
hates to argue?

How it molds itself into
the shape of the pour,
makes a home where it lands,

but also never gives up its identity.

As if to say, "Sure, I'll stay
but only if I can be myself."

I think there is a lesson here.

# Selk *verb*

selk  |  \ selk \

## Definition of *selk*:

**1**    : to give yourself advice

## Throughout most of my childhood

I spoke with a stutter.

My mouth and my mind,
two people with no rhythm,
trying to teach the other how to dance.

I had to concentrate just to say
the simplest things.

When there is a struggle
inside the pulse of every word,

you understand that speaking
is a badge of honor

that some of us have
to fight for.

## Seventeen

If you find an old calendar,
strap it to a hospital bed, tie it down by its weekends,

and then C-section the belly of 1999.
There, you'll find a 17-year-old me

back when I was a tsunami
of awkward moments splashing
against a shoreline called Rochelle Moss

—A young lady who introduced my jaw to the floor
whenever she floated into 1st period—

This girl was a dandelion seed straddling a wish,
a dream I never thought would turn flesh and grin.

But wire hangers like me,
we don't become captain of the football team.

The only thing we are good at is stopping ourselves from saying
"I like you," to a girl that holds the remote control to our smiles.

We are blurry silhouettes against the backdrop of popular,
often wearing our skin like a costume of someone

we don't feel comfortable pretending to be.
We swallow earthquakes and tremble at the smell of perfume,
we are bashful, tongue-tied, and nervous in high definition.

When I was a senior in high school,
I was a pocket full of chalk dust.

I was elevator music on a CD that stuttered like a Volkswagen
with a really bad transmission. At this age, I was a ballot box

stuffed full of everyone's opinions except my own, and
my swagger was like watching a Walkman
trying to swallow a DVD.

At 17, I walked as if I was concerned
with how the ground would feel about my footsteps.

If I could find a way to write a letter to that boy,
that old sweater with itchy sleeves that I will grow out of,

I would say, "There will be days when you feel like a peacock
without feathers. You will feel flightless
and undeserving of attention.
But listen, you have to stop getting out of bed like an oil spill.
You're not a flat tire at 2 am. Stop acting like an accident.
You are not an accident. You're an apple on a pine tree
in a room full of lemons, and you come from a long line of

Swiss Army Pocketknives. Men who are small, sharp,
and dangerous when not handled carefully."

Some days, I wish my arms were 12 years long.
So I could reach all the way back there,
grab you by the shoulders, and say,
"When you see Rochelle Moss at the senior prom,

ignore the washing machine in your stomach,
tell her she looks beautiful tonight.

Extend your arm like a drawbridge
to a castle no one has visited in years
and say, *Will you dance with me?*"

II

The following words do not currently exist in the English language, but they should:

Abnermedium
Grest
Acentate
Primoris

# Perfect (Erasure)

by Ed Sheeran

I found ▮▮▮▮▮▮

▮▮▮▮▮▮▮▮▮▮

▮▮▮▮▮▮

▮▮▮▮▮▮▮▮▮▮▮▮

▮▮▮▮▮▮▮▮▮▮▮▮▮▮

▮▮▮▮▮▮▮▮▮▮▮▮

▮▮▮▮▮▮

▮▮▮▮▮▮

▮▮▮▮▮▮▮▮▮▮▮▮▮▮

▮▮▮▮▮▮▮▮▮

▮▮▮▮▮▮▮▮▮▮▮▮▮▮▮▮

▮▮▮▮▮▮▮▮▮ our favorite song

▮▮▮▮▮▮▮▮ whispered underneath ▮▮▮▮

▮▮▮▮▮▮▮▮▮▮▮

▮▮▮▮▮▮▮▮▮▮▮▮▮▮

▮▮▮▮▮▮▮▮▮▮▮▮▮▮▮▮▮

▮▮▮▮▮▮▮▮▮▮ secrets

▮▮▮▮▮▮▮ of our own

▮▮▮▮▮▮

▮▮▮▮▮▮▮

▮▮▮▮▮

▮▮▮▮▮▮

▮▮▮▮▮▮

▮▮▮▮▮▮▮▮▮▮▮▮▮▮

▮▮▮▮▮▮▮▮▮▮▮▮▮

▮▮▮▮▮▮▮▮ beautiful.

▮▮▮▮▮▮▮ tonight

██ , I'm dancing in the dark with you ██████████

██████████████████████████████████████

████████████

██████ an angel █████

███████████

I don't deserve ██

██████████

# Abnermedium *noun*

ab · ner · me · di · um  |  \ ab-nər-mē-dē-əm \

## Definition of *abnermedium*:

**1**   : one who rejects something that they know is actually good for them

# You are a strange kind of beautiful

The type of magic
foolish men run from

and run back to
when it's too late.

## How

did you learn to live without me?

Your absence became
a classroom.

## If you find yourself

tucked into the corner of morning
and your smile has too many thorns
and loneliness is a rumor your thoughts
are spreading about your bones

if you have the unshakable urge
to reach out for something
and have no idea what it is

possibly

I am somewhere
doing the exact same thing.

# **Grest** *noun*

grest | \ grest \

## Definition of *grest*:

1    : someone whose presence brings you joy
2    : a person that makes you happy without doing anything out of the
     ordinary

## When you walk into the room

my mouth becomes a cathedral
of imperfect teeth,

my entire jaw locks into
a prayer circle,

my smile turns 7 am
and morphs a choir of fireflies.

I hope to sing forever
like this.

# **Acentate** *verb*

a · cen · tate  |  \ a-sen-tāt \

## Definition of *acentate*:

**1**     : to take a picture that you think is perfect

## I hope the camera gods
## bless you with a steady hand

great lighting, the perfect angle,
and enough storage space
to save the results.

May you snap the picture
at the right time, eyes open
and smiling with your entire face.

Months from now,
I hope you stumble
across the picture

and you are ambushed
by your own radiance.

# **Primoris** *verb*

pri · mor · is  |  \ prī-mər-is \

## Definition of *primoris*:

**1**     : to see the love of your life for the first time

# A lot like you

My grandmother once told me
that she believes the average girl
begins to plan her wedding at the age of 7.

Tells me that she picks the colors and the cake first.
By the age of 10, she knows the time and location.
By 17, she's already chosen a gown
and a maid of honor. By 23,
she's waiting for someone who doesn't break out in hives
when they hear the word "commitment—"

Someone who doesn't smell like a Band-Aid
drenched in lonely—.
Someone who isn't a temporary solution to the empty
side of the bed—.
Someone who will hold her hand like it's the only one
they've ever seen.

To be honest,
I don't know what kind of tux I'll be wearing.
I have no clue what my wedding will look like,
but, I imagine,
the woman who pins my last name to hers
will butterfly down the aisle like a 5-foot-promise.
I imagine,
her smile will be so large that you'll see it on Google Maps
and know exactly where our wedding is being held.

The woman that I plan to marry
will have champagne in her walk,
and I will get drunk on her footsteps.
When the pastor asks
if I take this woman to be my wife,
I will say "Yes" before they finish the sentence.

I'll apologize later for being impolite,
but I will also explain
that our first kiss happened 6 years ago,
and I've been practicing my "Yes,"
for the past 2,165 days.
When people ask me about my wedding,
I never really know what to say.
But when they ask me about my future wife—

I always tell them:
"Her eyes are the only Christmas lights
that deserve to be seen all year long."
I tell them,
"If my alarm clock sounded like her voice,
my snooze button would collect dust."
I tell them,
"If she came in a bottle,
I would drink her until my vision is blurry
and my friends take away my keys.
If she was a book,
I would memorize her table of contents;
I would read her cover to cover."

Hoping to find typos,
just so we can both have a few things to work on.
Because, aren't we all unfinished?

## Golden Girls Theme Song (Erasure)

Thank You For Being A Friend
By Andrew Gold & Cynthia Fee

█████ you █████████████ ,
█████████ a road █████ ██████
████████████████████████████████
██████████████████████
████████████████████████
██████████ , ████████████████████████
██████████ a party.
██████████ you ████
████ , ████████████ the biggest gift ████████████████
And the card ████████████████
██████████████████████ .
█████ you ████████████████ ,
████████████████████████
██████████████ a friend
█████████████
██████████████████████
████████████████████████████████
██ not ashamed to ██
██████████████████████
████████████████ stand up and take a bow
██████████████████████
████████████████████
████████████████████████
██████████████████

# III

The following words do not currently exist in the English language, but they should:

Parlee
Admonus
Nescium
Nomortice
Brevis
Solosum
Mutanom
Sepheegrum
Perdit

## Miranda Rights (Erasure)

"You have the right to remain silent. ███████ you ██ can ██████ be used against you in a court of law. You ███████████████ ██████ cannot afford an attorney, ██████████████████████.

# It is the year 2036

and yes,
J-Lo still looks amazing.

Morgan Freeman still looks like . . .
Morgan Freeman.

Lil Wayne is 53. He still drinks lean
and recently started telling everyone
that he invented hip hop.

It is an election year.
Beyoncé is the Democratic Presidential
Nominee, and her campaign slogan is
"To the left to the left."

Conversate is officially a word;
skurtskurt is also a word.

On TV, there are commercials asking if you
drank Four Loko in the 2010's, because
you might qualify for financial compensation.

Popeyes just brought back the chicken sandwich,
Chick-fil-A responds by opening on Sundays
and McDonald's finally fixed the ice cream machine.

Arby's went out of business 10 years ago,
and no one has noticed.

Candy corn is illegal,
Milky Ways are also illegal,
but you can still buy guns at Walmart.
We had a mass shooting last week,
and it wasn't even on the news.

We still write poems about racism.
Most of the police force has been
replaced with drones.

Unarmed black people are still being killed, but
now it's called a mechanical error.

# Parlee *verb*

par · lee  |  \ pär-lē \

## Definition of *parlee*:

**1**    : to tell the truth knowing it will make others uncomfortable

## Speak

because your
voice is currency,

and their comfort isn't worth
your silence.

# NRA Statement on Texas, Ohio Tragedies

FAIRFAX, Va.—Our deepest sympathies are with the families and victims of these tragedies, as well as the entire communities of El Paso and Dayton. On behalf of our millions of members, we salute the courage of the first responders and others offering their services during this time.

The NRA is committed to the safe and lawful use of firearms by those exercising their Second Amendment freedoms. We will not participate in the politicizing of these tragedies but, as always, we will work in good faith to pursue real solutions that protect us all from people who commit these horrific acts.

# NRA Statement on Texas, Ohio Tragedies (Erasure)

these

firearms

will not

protect us

from horrific acts.

# Click

There are 2 things I know
about people and guns:

they both feel strange
when you hold them
for the 1st time,

and something always clicks
when they are empty.

## Climate Change

Last week,
I randomly stumbled across a list of products
available in other countries
but illegal in the U.S. because they are too dangerous.

Things like
puffer fish and ackee fruit.

I heard the next product that will be banned
is the plastic straw.

The plastic isn't biodegradable;
instead of recycling, people often just throw them away.
They end up in landfills and oceans,
and I believe this is important.

The last time I went to a concert,
I couldn't focus on the music.
I spent the first 45 minutes analyzing all the exits,
scanning the room, trying to see if I could find anybody
who wasn't happy to be there,
anybody who looked like they might be comfortable
turning a good time into a crime scene,
anybody who wouldn't mind
transforming an entire room of strangers
into a pop-up cemetery full of people
who just so happen to like the same songs.

A shooter always seems obvious in the aftermath.
After we hear what happened,
after his photo is released.
Devin is 25.
He stopped going to the Waffle House in Nashville
after a man walked in with a semi-automatic rifle.

Brittany is 41.
She decided to home-school her daughter
after the shooting at Stoneman Douglas.

Adam is 27.
He stopped going to clubs after Omar Mateen
killed 49 people at Pulse in Orlando
and now I'm wondering,
when can we say
this is also the environment?

In 1988, after 6-thousand people
were injured by lawn darts,
we made them illegal,

but guns have killed 30-thousand people
every year in this country.

Now,
preschools are having Active Shooter Drills.
Now,
more high schools are installing metal detectors.
Now,
we're talking about giving guns to the teachers
so they can protect the students,

but that's like burning all the trees in the spring
so the forest fire won't take them in the summer.
America, this is climate change.

# Admonus *verb*

ad · mon · us  |  \ ad-mä-nəs \

## Definition of *admonus*:

**1**     : when someone who is considered dangerous does something to remind you of their humanity

## I watched the viral video of the police officer

playing basketball.

Finally,
a shooting

that doesn't need
a burial.

# Nescium *noun*

ne · sci · um  |  \ 'ne si əm \

Definition of *nescium*:

1      : a living thing that does not know it is being preyed upon


# Nomortice *noun*

no · mor · tice  |  \ nō-mȯr-təs \

Definition of *nomortice*:

1      : a movie where no one dies

## Alternate endings for the black movies that I can't stop watching

In *Menace to Society*:

The drive by happens
an hour too late
and the bullets are
all dressed up for nothing.
Cane moves to Atlanta with Ronnie,
he works nights and watches her son
while she's in class.

*Boyz in the Hood*:

The day gives Ricky
back to his family.
He makes it home,
decides to go to USC,
plays for 3 years, and gets drafted
by the Raiders.

*Training Day*:

Denzel pays the Russians,
they call it even and he retires from
the police force 5 years later.

He plays golf, takes up gardening,
writes a letter to Hoit saying,
"You did the right thing."

*New Jack City*:

Neno Brown doesn't kill Gee Money.
He packs all 10 years of their relationship

into one hug, lets him go, sheds a tear.
And they never speak again.

If the movie says,
"Our life is more
important than our death"

Will we pay money
just to see black people

living?

## When they say he is black

When they say he was unarmed—
When they say he was killed—

When they say the officer's name—
When they show his face—
When the system
licks his fingers clean.

When they say there is no crime
underneath his fingernails—
you realize the phrase
"Life is short"
sounds a little different
when you are being hunted.

# Instructions for black people

Speak. I dare you. Say something.
Say nothing. Be silent.
Be a stone. Be a Polaroid.
Be anything that doesn't make a sound. Your tongue
is a firearm on a plane.
Watch your mouth.
Watch your temper.
Watch your attitude. Watch "Rosewood,"
watch "Fruitvale Station,"
watch us kill people who look like you
and get away with it. Watch the news.
Watch your back.

Don't wear hoodies,
don't wear T-shirts,
don't wear jeans or sneakers.
Pull up your pants.
Tie your shoes.

Don't whistle.
don't sing,
don't smile, laugh, or frown.
Don't stare.

Don't look away. Look at me.
Look at me. Look at me. Look
at me. Don't drive

or walk or run.
Don't run—
we like our targets
better still.

You thought I was just a country?

I'm a record player.
Watch me put on history
and spin it backwards.

# **Brevis** *verb*

bre · vis  |  \ bre-vis \

## Definition of *brevis*:

**1**    : to try to become friends with someone or something that only wants to hurt them

## To the Black Donald Trump Supporters

Remember
when Rafiki
held Simba in the air?

Remember
how the zebras celebrated?

Remember
how the antelopes were cheering?

As if they had no idea
what happens
when a lion gets hungry.

A meal
cannot be friends
with a mouth,

especially when
it's feeding time.

It's always

feeding time.

# Solosum *verb*

so · lo · sum  |  \ sō-lō-səm \

## Definition of *solosum*:

**1**  : to be the only person in the room that isn't white

## Let's just say

I am the only one
at this party that
has no idea what
sunburn feels like.

I put on cocoa butter
before I left the house,
and I wonder if they
can smell it on my hands.

I had chicken on Wednesday,
and I think they know.

Biggie starts to play
everyone yells, "I love this song,"
and, suddenly, anxiety picks up a hammer
and builds condos that are too
expensive for my peace to live inside of.

I hear, "If you don't know
now you know," and I hope
the speaker malfunctions.

The room spins, the pause
seems a lot longer than normal,
and this is the kind of loneliness
that turns all the oxygen into quicksand.

Biggie is about to say, "Nigga,"
and I'm wondering if he's the only one.

# Mutanom  *verb*

mut · a · nom  |  \ mut-ə-näm \

## Definition of *mutanom*:

**1**   : to change the name of something to make people think it's different

## I remember when this neighborhood was an orchard

Every tree
was an endless bloom
and wore its newest apples,

but the block's been turned
to cider,

poured into a fancy bottle,
they changed the name

and called something
the locals can't pronounce.

# **Sepheegrum** *noun*

se · phee · grum  |  \ sə-fi-grəm \

## Definition of *sepheegrum*:

**1**    : a person who is pardoned for terrible acts, typically because they are famous or associated with something positive

## The youth choir sings
## "I believe I can fly"

"Step in the name of love"
comes on at the wedding.

"Ignition the remix"
plays during the barbecue.

The room becomes a jukebox
and just like that,
we forget Aaliyah was 15.

Just like that,
the video of the 14-year-old girl disappears.

Interesting, how accountability
becomes a set of clumsy hands
that only close when they have
no other options.

Interesting, how
a man's transgressions can easily
turn into dust,

as long as he makes a melody
that we can dance to

and only harms black women.

# **Perdit** *verb*

per · dit  |  \ per-dit \

## Definition of *perdit*:

**1**   : to grow in a place that you aren't supposed to

## The Peace Lily

is a flower that can
grow and survive
even if it's left
in the shade.

See?

We don't always
choose our environment,

but we can't let that
stop us from blooming.

The following words do not currently exist in the English language, but they should:

Vamri
Coliber
Skelt

# Family Matters Theme Song (Erasure)
As Days Go By
By Jesse Frederick, Bennet Salvay & Scott Roeme

It's a rare ▇▇▇▇▇▇▇▇▇
▇▇▇▇▇▇▇▇▇▇
▇▇▇▇▇▇▇
▇▇▇▇▇▇▇▇

▇▇▇▇▇▇▇▇▇▇ magic ▇ inside ▇ gentle walls.
▇▇▇▇▇▇ a tower of ▇▇▇
real love burstin' out of every seam.

▇▇▇
▇▇▇ our house ▇▇▇▇
▇▇▇▇ ,
▇▇▇▇▇▇ the blues with tenderness.

▇▇▇
▇▇▇
▇▇
▇▇▇▇

▇▇▇
▇▇▇▇

## Dear PTSD

I've always wondered
what my dad was like
before he met you.

## Whoever said a choir

has to be more than 2 people,

obviously had never been in a car
with my father and me.

When Bob Marley is on the radio,
somehow, we become the same age.

The stereo is loud, but we sing louder.
This is how we safeguard the memory of us,

how we challenge Alzheimer's to a fist fight,
how we snarl at the disease—

Just to make sure it knows
that we will not go quietly.

## Lasalle

My brother is the toughest flower
in my mother's garden.

A gentle giant
with copper hands,

John Henry folklore
with an alternate ending.

In this version of the story
the machine breaks,
and he does not.

My brother, Lasalle Francisco,
fable and comic book strong.

I once watched him
bring all the groceries
from the car in one trip.

He once threw me in the air
so high, when I landed,

I was 2 years older.

## It usually happens

right before
I become a spill of laughter.

The serious breaks—
my entire face cracks open—

my mouth—an egg smashing
its own body against the edge
of a frying pan—and now I am
sunny side up.

This smile is the first gift my
mother gave me.

A present that unwraps
itself in public places
without my permission.

I unfurl into a grin, and
there she is.

Simeona Francisco,

A woman who doesn't
believe in bad days.

She calls the rain
a carwash.

# Vamri *verb*

vam · ri  |  \ vam-ri \

## Definition of *vamri*:

**1**    : to substitute the words "I love you" with another phrase

## Uwani

We don't say "I love you"
very often, but we do say
"Have you eaten today?"

I imagine, somewhere,
in an alternate universe,

There is a language
where those 2 things
have the same meaning.

# Coliber *verb*

col · i · ber  |  \ kȯ-lə-bər \

## Definition of *coliber*:

**1**   : to cook without needing instructions

## The women in my family never use measuring cups

or tablespoons.

They say, "Season it
until it tastes good,"
"Add some butter," "Make sure
there's enough cheese," and
"Cook it until it's ready."

Somehow, the dish always
comes to the table

wearing its best clothes.

# Isn't She Lovely (Erasure)

By Stevie Wonder

Isn't she ███████

████████████████████

████████████████

Less than one minute old.

████████████████████████████████

Making ██████████████████

███████████████████████████████

████████████████

███ the ██████ best

████████████████████████████

██████████████ Heaven ████████.

████████████████████████████

██████████████████████ life ██████

████████████████████████████████

████████████████

████████████████████████

████ is ████████

[1]The meaning of her name.

████████████████████████████

████████████████████████████

████████████████████████████████████

─────────────

1. Zoey means Life and is of Greek origin

## Unsolicited advice

for men who become fathers
while they are still trying to raise themselves.

When she calls

and her voice is a house
next to a train track and shakes with every word,

remove the locomotive from your tone
and say, "Hello."

When she says she is going into labor,
don't make a joke about unions,
don't get angry,
save the fire for another time.
It makes no sense to torch the entire grove,
knowing you will have to live in the trees.
Turn the car around. Your daughter will
be born in 10 hours, so go to the hospital.

Call Javon, call Terisa, call Imani;
put "Everything is Going to be Alright" on repeat
and call it a gospel.
Call it a prediction.
When you get there,
take a deep breath
and walk in.

When her brother hugs you,
hug him back.
When he asks if you're ok,
say "yes" or "no."
Both of those answers are correct.

Don't turn into a windshield.
Don't crack. Don't shatter.
You can't believe that God has a plan
and also believe in accidents.

When you see her father,
shake his hand and introduce yourself.

Say your name like it means something,
hug her mother like she is your own.
They are all your family now.

When Zoey comes out of the womb,
don't pass out,
don't vomit.
Grab the scissors,
cut the umbilical cord,
and hold her in your arms.

When she cries,
sing her a song;
something by Bob Marley.

I suggest
"Everything is Going to Be Alright."

# Skelt *verb*

skelt | \ skelt \

## Definition of *skelt*:

**1**    : to interrupt a conversation with a tasteless joke

# I say black fatherhood

He, with a voice soaked in privilege,
drags a joke through the conversation,
says, "that's kind of an oxymoron, right?
You know black . . . fatherhood. Get it?"

So . . . Anybody who knows me, knows
my hands are two pots that are always
full of water

and, sometimes,
my temper is a gasoline stove
only a few people know how to turn off.

When he said it,
I clenched my fist so hard,
I thought I saw steam leaking through my fingers.

I wanted to swing,
I wanted to turn his face into a meal,

but instead

I said

*Zoey.*

*Zoey.*

And my daughter's name became two ice cubes
in my hands:

the only thing that stopped them from boiling over.

## Zoey

4 years ago,
if you were to ask me
how big the world is,
I would have guessed around
30 thousand miles.

If you asked me today,
I would say,
3 feet tall, 16 pounds.

So small,
you can pick it up
with your hands.

## and the morning
## shows up

again,
like it always does—


a reminder that each day
comes with free refills.

I tell myself that every hour
is happy hour, as long as I am
on this side of the ground,

and maybe that's a good
enough reason to smile
and get out of bed.

I know it's not the weekend,
but Friday and Saturday are
watching—

Let's give them something
to talk about.

# Index

# Acknowledgements

Thank you to my family. My parents, Samuel and Simeona, my siblings, Uwani and Lasalle, my uncle Pine, aunt Yolly, my cousins Rassan and Jameel. All these poems are also yours because you have shaped the way I look at the world.

Thank you to the Micael family; Micael, Saba, Degol, Maezn, Ghebriel, Semhar and, the mother of my daughter, Samra.

Thank you to my poetry family.

Collective Purpose: Jessica Molina, Anthony Blacksher, Thali, Viet Mai, Kendrick Dial, and Chris Wilson. You all nurtured and supported me, you all saw my potential and told me how endless my possibilities are.

Da Poetry Lounge: Shihan Van Clef and Javon Johnson. You are my brothers and my mentors. Thank you so much for taking me under your wings and encouraging me to work harder.

Thank you to Imani Cezanne, Terisa Siagatonu, and T Miller. You are my sisters. Thank you for all the ways you show up for me and also hold me accountable.

Fiveology: Javon, Andrew Tyree, Shawn William, and Prentice Powell. We've all almost fought each other, fought for each other, and you are a part of some of the most memorable moments in my life.

San Diego Slam: Natasha Hooper, Anita D, Amen Ra, Cole Lawson, and Chrissy Croft. You all have inspired me to become a better artist and re-energized our entire community. I am so excited to see what the future has for you.

Krystal and Eric Fountain. You've been in the audience since Spoken Word Wednesday's at Alliant and you're still supporting. I can't thank you enough.

Thank you to my daughter, Zoey. You are the best part of every day. You've saved my life so many times and you don't even know it. You make me want to be a better human. I love you so much.

Last but not least, thank you to Button Poetry (again) for this amazing opportunity.

**Rudy Francisco** is one of the most recognizable names in Spoken Word Poetry. Rudy Francisco has shared stages with prominent artists such as Gladys Knight, Jordin Sparks, Musiq Soulchild, and Jill Scott. Ultimately, Rudy's goal is to continue to assist others in harnessing their creativity while cultivating his own. Rudy Francisco is the author of "Helium." He is also an Individual World Poetry Slam Champion, a National Poetry Slam Champion and appeared on NBC's "The Tonight Show" starring Jimmy Fallon.

# OTHER BOOKS BY BUTTON POETRY

If you enjoyed this book, please consider checking out some of our others, below. Readers like you allow us to keep broadcasting and publishing. Thank you!

Available at buttonpoetry.com/shop and more!